The Art of Patience, Gratitude & Courage

This book is dedicated to my mom Gina, my brother Matteo, my uncle Miguel and my late father, Manuel. As well as all the rest of my extended family, friends and supporters across the globe.

Thank you for your endless support, inspiration and guidance in helping me become who I was meant to be.

Table of Contents

Introduction

Greetings and thank you for choosing this book.

I'd love to introduce myself but I'm going to save all of the formalities for the end. For now, I want you to keep an open mind to the possibility that you're reading this for a reason and a purpose.

I'm going to take a shot in the dark here by assuming you're either searching for answers to a very specific problem, or you're just looking to improve an area of yourself which you know has more room for growth.

Perhaps you were curious, simply bored or maybe someone recommended this to you. Maybe the front cover grabbed your attention. No matter how you arrived at this point, you're here now.

And if there's something I'm absolutely certain of is that you'll find a bit of wisdom after reading through the pages.

Before getting started, I'd like to make some things as clear as day for you. That way, any initial doubts or questions get addressed immediately and you'll gain some peace of mind knowing that you're in the correct place. Even if you still have a few burning questions afterwards, you'll find the answers in the pages that follow this introduction.

This is a humble approach.

The purpose of this is to share with you the three most important core values that I take into consideration every single day. These are values that can upgrade your life if you're already focused on them, and can also be easily adopted by virtually anyone who thinks they don't already have them.

This is a method I've been exercising on my own, with all of my personal relationships and professional interactions with unmatched success in comparison to the other things I've attempted.

As you read in the title, I can almost guarantee you're already applying these values on a daily basis, with or without your knowledge. If that is the case, let this book serve as a reinforcement with fresh perspectives.

In case this is your first time learning about how to incorporate these values into your day to day life, I'm glad you're here with an open mind. Through mastery of each one, you'll begin to understand how they are a part of everything you'll encounter along your journey.

On the other end of the spectrum, what has worked for me and others still may not work for you. Therefore, I'm making no claims that this is the *only* solution in the world, unlike many others tend to do.

As a matter of fact, it's not really a solution at all, though you may choose to see it as such.

You see, there's no darker secret to unearth beyond what you get here in these pages. There are no bells and whistles to this and you won't find any slimy sales pitch at the end of this either, as I'm sure you've encountered many times before.

With that said, the expectation is that you use the knowledge I've collected here to create your own informed decisions. Or you can also reject what I'm saying and that should help you along just as well. That's the idea: to get you thinking and moving.

It's also worth noting that I mention some things surrounding one's health but this isn't a replacement for medical advice. You must do your due diligence and seek the right help should you feel you need it.

All in all, I'm just a man who has led quite an eventful life, sharing something that aims to help you navigate through chaos, bring out the most of your limited life experience and do so in the simplest way I've found.

This is an unconventional approach.

I'm keeping things informative and as easy to understand as possible. This is a book I've wanted to put together for the everyday reader for some time now and isn't meant to be too difficult to digest.

Therefore, I'm not here to show off my lexical dominance or fill every other paragraph with statistics and academic studies pretending I did all of the work.

My expertise is mainly experiential and I don't want to just regurgitate numbers or quote studies that you can easily find through an online search. I definitely encourage you to conduct your own proper investigation to verify the effectiveness of this method if you want to do so.

The thing is that I've read several books that place far too much focus on research which is mostly conducted in clinical or other types of controlled settings. This isn't to say that I'm against data that supports the types of arguments I'm outlining. On the contrary, it always helps.

The reason I'm going rogue and breaking away from that traditional delivery of this kind of information is because life isn't a controlled environment.

Therefore, my tactics will be a bit more unorthodox as well. That is exactly why I'm taking the slightly anecdotal, guerrilla approach.

Basically, I'm a storyteller. I'm not a rocket surgeon or a mystic.

I chose this path in hopes of reaching those of you who are seeking answers but would otherwise get lost in or intimidated by the pages of any other formally written document.

This is simplicity at its finest.

One thing this book isn't aiming for is to pile more things on top of what's already on your plate.

In fact, this will help you realize how much you can achieve with less and still maintain your quality of life across multiple areas despite any circumstance. This is how you can learn to never lose sight of your goals, remain in the moment and still remember where you can always return to should you ever need to adjust your course.

In essence, this is a short guide explaining the simple psychology behind a method that you can use in everyday life.
It's a way to eliminate unnecessary stress by applying practical minimalism, stoic ideas and other philosophies.

Lastly, through recognition of these values and their conversion into faculties, you'll finally be able to take meaningful action in a direction that is ideal for you.

The beautiful thing about it is that it'll also allow you to see both sides of the coin. This means, you'll find it easily accessible during times of turmoil and times of joy alike. The primary focus will remain on how to endure chaos more effectively. Still, we won't neglect the benefit of this in times of peace and prosperity.

I'll be detailing each value as thoroughly as possible while keeping things light so you may come back to this whenever you need it.

With all of that out of the way, let's begin the journey.

The Noise Trap

Let me paint a picture for you.

Imagine for a moment you're struggling with money management. The bills are stacking higher and each paycheck keeps getting burned on all the debts that are owed. This stress is only multiplied each time a debt collector calls your phone from random numbers every other hour of the day or sends the same notices in the mail over and over again.

This makes simple things like answering the phone and checking your mailbox slightly more tormenting than other tasks.

Your method of transportation works just fine outside of needing the occasional service here and the additional part there. Despite all of this, you still have a roof over your head and you're still able to put food on the table for your family.

However, trying to make ends meet by working more and more makes it increasingly difficult to take a much needed vacation to breathe a little.

On top of that, you begin to have difficulty building or maintaining interpersonal relationships. Striking that next business partnership to increase your earnings seems almost like an unfathomable goal.

Even having a simple conversation with friends and family has become exhausting.

There are no longer many things to talk about besides work, how little you slept through the week or another tragedy on television.

At this point, you consider picking up a few courses to learn about public speaking or tap into body language skills in order to help yourself. This could make you more marketable to potential employers. Having to manage your studies, work and personal life prove to be challenging all on their own.

As if all of that wasn't enough, now you're hit with unexpected health problems. Some take just a quick fix, others cause you daily discomfort and pain. Visits to the clinic, picking up prescriptions at the pharmacy and worrying about what's to come naturally stress you out more each passing day.

And the cycle continues...

You're probably thinking that's some terrible luck for one person to have.

While all of these problems along with several others that go unmentioned are certainly not the worst of the worst, they're a reality that many of us battle with daily.

Continuing on, let's say you're facing one or many of these challenges. You're likely to find yourself in a desperate hunt for answers from any possible source.

Maybe you go about it by asking friends for advice or researching different topics, watching videos online, turning towards family, trying out a few different methods, etc.

If you're fortunate, you now have a wide range of options to choose from to be able to handle your problems. There's a catch though.

The answers you find may only lead to more complications in both the short and long term. You probably have run into as many solutions as you have problems. Some call it "analysis paralysis". Truth is, in the search for new solutions, it's easy to chip away at one wall while another is slowly creeping up right next to it.

Inevitably, having no means to organize yourself or your thoughts after gathering so much information will leave you drained of energy, drained of useful resources, and in the worst of cases, drained of hope. That last one is where things can turn dangerous.

Thankfully, the human spirit is a force to be reckoned with.

This means that you can always hop back on the horse and ride back out into the sunset.

Hunting down more answers to more problems as they arise, adding more weapons to your arsenal of knowledge.

So you can continue charging forward, crossing tasks off the lists and tackling all of the challenges in front of you. Continuously doing this helps you reinvigorate that burning fire you have inside to find your true path.

Your eyes are transfixed by the beauty of the mountain top ahead. You can almost hear all of the modern-day online gurus screaming that, you too, can achieve all your dreams, have the fancy sports car, the beach house and be anywhere in the world with just a one-time payment of $997.

Because you've been on such a long search for the one answer to all of your problems, the lucrative promises of health and wealth keep you trudging on strong and relentless. Hopefully, each step you take doesn't take a bit of wind from your sails with it.

Through perseverance and a bit of luck, it's true that you just may reach your goals and are finally able to look beyond troubling times...

Or maybe you're completely burned out, confused and find yourself stumbling time after time. Doomed to repeat this dreaded cycle.

If you can relate to any of this, what I'm getting ready to explain will make a lot more sense.

I painted the aforementioned picture for you because those were all of the things that myself and others have endured in the past.

This further proved that I had to develop and implement something on my own. At the time, it seemed that the people I was turning towards to help me with my confusion were confused themselves.

Nothing seemed to be working for me until I begun eliminating what wasn't working for me.

What I noticed is that this is something that isn't often discussed, especially at the time of this writing.

It turned into the only way I'd be able to make a breakthrough in my personal journey and aid others in discovering the correct direction to aim for in theirs.

Let's keep digging through the layers so you can better understand what I mean by the examples I just noted.

The first step is as follows.

Stop Shouting.

In an age where the world's information is virtually accessible from anywhere you have a cell phone signal or an internet connection, and every single person you know bombards you with unsolicited answers to problems you didn't even know you had, it has become that much easier to get lost in a sea of disruptive noise.

We all have our own problems at different stages and different turning points in our lives.

Now, depending on your most pressing issue there's bound to be a myriad of valuable information and misinformation out there for you to endlessly consume. This could deal with a number of topics varying from how to become healthier to how to care for a pet spider or how to start an indoor garden.

Oftentimes you'll find several books, videos and articles that have a lot of great information. Unfortunately, some of it will also contain conflicting information.

You're probably thinking this book is no exception to that statement, and you would be right. I recognize I don't have all of the answers and some of them may seem contradicting. There is however a certain amount of calculated risk, hence I'm here to present this case so you may reconsider your stance.

Another thing I wanted to mention is that it's not all that terrible running into conflicting information.
If you look closer, it can be wonderfully useful to come up with your own answers through the process of elimination and critical thinking. Likewise, I understand how it can also feel like an endless search in the wrong direction.

I wouldn't be surprised if this constant back and forth in the wrong directions caused a large portion of your days to be spent in search of the right guidance to kick start your self-improvement.

You've probably spent weeks, if not months, with field experts trying to figure out your next power moves.
A few other examples of the search for answers could include deciding on changing your career in an attempt to break the daily routine, earn more money, have a better title, or gain a different sense of purpose.

Looking at it from a social perspective, using applications for dating or joining social groups may have also crossed your radar when you were looking to make sense of things.

Or perhaps, you're the type that likes to go at it alone and try your luck at discovering something that works for you when embarking on your unique journey.

The choices are limitless, meaning the noise of the modern world is now louder than ever.

I've gone down many paths, turning many stones along the way in search of meaning and purpose. Believe me when I tell you that I know just how overwhelming all of this can become when you throw in the unpredictability of life itself.

What you'll notice with that is you'll always have constant conflict. You may be lucky enough to push past conflict with ease and carry on. Other times, you may feel like you're stuck. No matter where you find yourself, the most important thing is to ensure that you're either trudging or struggling through the right path.

With all of that in mind, I'd like to remind you that the seemingly endless search for happiness and fulfillment in itself is an admirable display of resilience. You may see these types of challenges and roadblocks as failures or mistakes, but as you already know they can also teach you very valuable lessons.

Inversely, I know how exhausting and infuriating things might get. It's like you're witnessing all of these opportunities just pass you by. Even the ones you finally manage to obtain come with their own set of drawbacks. It's frustrating, and that's normal.

Fret not, you're not alone when negative emotions take over.

In fact, despite these emotions or sensations clouding your better judgment, I still encourage you to sit with them and feel them through. Negative emotions shouldn't be something you demonize in yourself or others. When you think it through, it's really the manner of expression that you're worried about. You'll learn exactly why that is soon enough.

Circling back, the only thing the noise you're subjecting yourself to is doing is setting you up for failure. This mental and emotional hijacking can happen in a matter of seconds, sometimes without you even realizing what's going on in that very moment.

The end result is that you react out of alignment with yourself and end up causing more harm than good to yourself, to others and also throw your life purpose out of balance. It's like trying to hear the song through the static on the radio.

The mission here is to eliminate that noise and bring you back to the ground. Better yet, you'll also realize that you don't even have to reduce the noise at all because you don't have to remain in the same room with it for any more time than is necessary. You can apply this regardless of your past, present or future challenges.

I'm positive you'll begin to see how greatly this method can benefit the process of attaining your goals, big or small. Some of the examples that I outlined will show you a comparison between the three values and their respective uses.

The majority of these examples will encompass professional relationships, relationships with others, and the relationship you have with yourself. The last one is easily the most important because if you can begin changing yourself, you'll be able to change the world around you.

The reason most of these examples will surround those three categories is because we want to narrow things down and keep the process simple. We can spend all our lives talking about every single little thing you'll experience like doing laundry, going to the beach, disciplining your kids, etc. I would have to write a book for each one. That's how much information there is to cover for all other scenarios.

Instead, you'll benefit more from knowing there will eventually come a time when you'll be working on something to contribute to your society or a professional collective. There will also be a time when you'll feel connected to other people on a deeper level than just superficial.

And even if you hypothetically never work a day in your life and don't ever wish to connect with anyone else, you'll introspect in some way or another as that is practically inescapable.

Out of all the examples I'll mention here, remember that we're using unconventional tactics against the noise of the world. So I'll go into just enough detail to understand, but also leave room to allow you to discover other daily uses and their potential benefits on your own after you're completely done with this.

The best part is that as you gain mastery over these values, you'll begin to notice just how similar the patterns of chaos and joy really are.

In return, you'll be able to keep calm more often, feel less stressed over things that normally would set you off and become a more balanced person than you already are now.

This means you'll achieve more meaningful things with less. You'll have the opportunity of becoming an exemplary member of your community. At the very least, you'll be the best version of yourself day in and day out and lead others by example.

Your willingness to learn this method will let you see things from a standpoint and perspective that seems to have been lost among all of this modern chaos and noisy environments.

The last piece of advice I have if you're someone who's already implementing the method I'm about to share is this: please keep in mind those who are not on your level yet.
I encourage you to share this with the people you think might be facing a difficult time adapting to chaos and help them perceive things from a different point of view. Work alongside them and understand that while it may not be

the best solution for them at this given time, it may just help them find the pieces they need to complete their puzzles.

The Noise Solution

Desperate times call for desperate measures.

It should come as no surprise that some people are more than capable of riding the storms of life like bats out of hell. Meanwhile, others are practically running around like chickens with their heads cut off. The question is: have you ever felt yourself falling into either of these two categories? Or have you ever communicated with someone that places you in either one of these categories? Almost like they preregister you with one of these labels?

With plenty of societal pressure almost forcing you to take a stand with either side, an even better question you could ask is why are these the only two choices available for your day to day engagements and survival?

The popular phrase "sink-or-swim" is the one that is more adequate for these kinds of situations.
This is the kind of mindset that's often adopted by the more hardened veterans of modern day life.

Now, it's no secret this mindset can be extremely effective in various scenarios. In retrospect, it was my personal favorite mindset when I was much younger, somewhere in my late teens and early twenties. I've no doubt that it has helped you at some point in time when fear, danger or maybe even mass confusion were prominent.

My only personal challenge with that "do o⁻ don't" mindset was that I couldn't snap out of it when I needed to so as to not cause any unintended harm to any innocent bystanders or someone I cared for. This happened because what I discovered about myself long ago is that even the slightest threatening situation always placed me in a defensive and aggressive state of mind. I didn't know how to stop myself or my thoughts from racing towards an immediate solution to a particular problem.

When I entered this mindset, I became more focused on being right than being happy, often to the point of trying to prove myself by working harder than I needed to at the office when it wasn't necessary, having shouting matches with other people anytime there was a slight disagreement between us and giving very few people, especially those close to me, the audience they yearned for when they needed it.
That's why sink-or-swim for me became one of my downfalls. By setting this unrealistic expectation for myself and others, it ended up being more destructive than constructive in my case.

Needless to say this ruined a lot of good opportunities for me because I was so stuck in "fight or flight" mode and I couldn't break free. I was in perpetual motion. So much so, that it got to the point where I didn't even know in what direction I was going anymore.

Once again, this begged the question: why were these the only two options for me and others?

I spent a few years breaking this down piece by piece to be able to fully grasp what was happening with me and to the people around me. After extensive research in the right direction and plenty of introspection, I found the answer to my problems and that of others to be so obvious, it was almost laughable.

I still believe sink-or-swim deserves credit. However, I've determined that it's more adequate and efficient if used as a secondary step in the grand scheme of the decision-making process.

In any case, whether you know this as fight-or-flight or sinking and swimming, as valuable as it can be, let's set all of it aside. The first core value you need to begin implementing immediately is your third option.
In a sink-or-swim world, I reintroduce the act of floating.

I: Patience

"It's your duty as a person of exemplary character to take your time, creatively express yourself and understand words in more ways than one."

Life will have an outstanding amount of challenges for all of us. This means that chaos and conflict are inevitable.

Wars will forever be waged between continents by politicians who don't realize the true extent of combat; sending many warriors and unsuspecting pacifists alike to the slaughterhouse. Friends and enemies will argue, bicker and tear into the beliefs and mindsets of one another in moments of weakness and emotional stress. Whether you like it or not, even you will battle against the little voice inside your mind from time to time.

Accepting that there will always be an opposite side to counter the weight of any kind of reality you find yourself in at any given moment is a daunting, but critical, first step in order to understand that you cannot have one without the other.

You wouldn't know yourself if it weren't for another. In essence, without chaos, you wouldn't know what peace would be.
That's why the phrase sink-or-swim holds a ton of truth for all intents and purposes. After all, how would you know what sinking feels like if you never swim and vice versa?

The idea behind floating, in this case patience, is to help you identify which of those two conflicting sides you'd rather be in to make more conscious choices to benefit you and others around you.

In other words, would you rather swim with the stream or against it? This is something you need to think about very carefully every chance you get. The easiest way to begin is as follows:

Stop Rushing Carelessly.

At the time of this writing, I've found that many of us are living in constant and persistent extremes. More often than not, you're doing too much or too little of any given thing, missing the point of floating entirely. Especially if you confuse patience with inaction.

You may argue that the line between these two terms is blurry. My counterargument is that there are stark differences between the two.

Simply put, inaction is a very finite choice. You've made the conscious choice to not act at all and remain permanently immobile, indecisive or stagnant.
This is akin to casting yourself into the sea. If you don't move at all, you will sink.

Patience has a brief moment of inaction but it doesn't mean the final choice has been made.

You're only calculating which choice to make. This is akin to wading in the water. So long as you flow in accordance with the waves, you'll stay afloat.

In this example, patience gives you the power to decide where to go from a place of stillness. Therein lies the difference.

Now, depending on the particular situation that you find yourself in, the amount of time it'll take you to make said choice will vary.

It might take you a few seconds, a couple of hours, a couple of days, etc. For example, it might take you less time to decide whether you want to speed past a yellow light than it would to decide what you'd like to eat for dinner at a restaurant after staring over the menu.

In the most extreme cases, it might take you an entire lifetime to make a particular decision on something. There is such a thing as patiently waiting forever for the right moment to act.

Not to say that there's anything necessarily wrong with the decision to remain inactive on something for the remainder of your natural life.

You're in absolute control of that thought, so long as you understand that the consequences of complete inaction can be grave. We'll cover the topic of consequence later on, but it's important to note for the sake of understanding how patience can be used beneficially and not detrimentally.

Patience is one of the most invaluable skills you can begin applying right this moment. You don't need any kind of special training or spend years trying to master it. You don't need any special equipment or anyone else to put it into practice with. You don't even need to finish reading this sentence.

You only need yourself and the moment you're in, and that moment is now.

The primary lesson behind patience is this. You need to consider taking the time to make your initial assessment of any situation you find yourself in, granted it's not immediate danger.
By observing your surroundings more carefully, you can begin to lessen the weight of any potential obstacle you're facing so that your next set of choices are clear and more effective.

Learning how to be completely still in the volatile unpredictability of chaotic events is vital for your own well-being. It will grant you the power necessary to dominate either side of said conflict should the need or want arise.

This is what gives you an edge over a large majority of others who are in constant motion and are prone to making rash decisions.

Easy enough? Let's make this even easier.

Ask yourself how many people do you know whom are capable of making decisions from a point of absolute clarity when they're near a mental, physical or emotional exhaustion point. Personally, I only know a handful. Though not impossible, it's definitely a very tough place to be in.

This happens to be the case for many people you'll encounter.

They're often angry or sad about something personal, just hungry or even tired when making the choices that they make.
It's possible that they may not even know how to take a pause and assess their surroundings or even themselves.

Not to mention, they just might not care to think of anything or anyone outside of themselves.
This puts those who they interact with at a disadvantage, since it's very difficult to make an irrational person see clearly. By mastering your own patience, you'll be capable of increasing the chances of withstanding unpredictable behavior.

You'll be able to bide your time and eventually come out on top whenever you confront the majority of situations in life.

To be more specific, you ideally want to be making choices when you're not experiencing negative emotions or sensations. It's also important to take all others into consideration whenever possible so as to ensure your decisions aren't having a negative impact on them.

When it comes to patience, another important thing to remember is that most of the time you're not required to take immediate action or remain in constant motion. Falling prey to the perception that taking a brief moment to assess your surroundings will end in complete disaster is downright foolish in the majority of situations that don't involve immediate danger or loss.

In other words, trying to match external action with equal or opposing action, quick or slow, large or small, won't always be the best answer if you have a misaligned energy behind your intention to act in the first place.

One way I can demonstrate this is when you're walking towards someone, and they end up trying to dodge you in the same direction that you try to dodge them. Now, you both end up doing this silly dance with one another, going left to right then right to left, mirroring each other's actions. You might get stuck here for a bit.

Instead of trying to match the action in this case, the solution is as simple as either one of you simply stopping, letting the other pass and carrying on.

Most of us are so eager to continue moving that we don't realize we end up wasting more energy and time by trying to cling on to it.

That's just one way of how this works. Other situations won't be so innocent. They might involve more serious repercussions therefore our moments of assessment should be more precise in determining our next set of moves. The last thing you want to do in dire situations is act recklessly, especially if the person or object in question is already doing that.

You mustn't overlook the power that patience and stillness hold over the constant crashing waves of everyday life.

I'm not going to too far as to discuss how you should be prioritizing your life decisions.
That's something you're responsible for and patience will help you achieve it, mainly through simple observation and open listening.
As the saying goes, it's more difficult to admire the colors of falling leaves from a moving vehicle than it is when standing still beneath the tree.

<u>Defining Patience</u>

What does patience mean to you?

I'm positive you often heard many people say they have no patience for certain things. I'm guilty of this as well. The truth is that everyone is capable of exercising patience, just in varying degrees.

As I mentioned before, this isn't something that requires any special training or equipment to unlock. You already possess this trait, it's innate. Even young children who seem to be in constant emotional disarray, throwing tantrums over toys that are taken away or have trouble communicating their feelings in the same way adults do are very capable of exercising patience to a degree that's mostly misunderstood to someone who's already mature.

What you must consider is that while everyone is capable of this, just like anything else, some might find it easier to do than others.

Some people are fortunate enough to have a natural talent to be able to bring out their best attributes in the face of adversity, while others just need the right guidance.

This is why learning to express yourself in more ways than one and understand others in more ways than one is so important.

One of the things you can begin doing is not shutting out the possibility of developing your ability to become more patient. It's not that you aren't patient at all, you just may need a little extra help. By saying you're "just not" patient, grateful, courageous, good-looking, intelligent, etc. you're pulling yourself back into the binary mentality of swimming-or-sinking.

To put it in another way, you're rushing into a decision before you even know where the decision will take you. It's like you're letting the decision make you and not the other way around, as it should be.

Think of it this way, telling yourself you're just not a patient person is like saying you're just not a swimmer. It's too finite of a statement, more relevant to preference rather than ability. It's statements such as these that act as the first brick of the mental walls you build for yourself, preventing you from taking meaningful action and making conscious choices to learn how to master these skills.

It sounds about as silly as saying you don't know how to sink, and that's about as easy as remaining inactive. Just don't do anything and it'll happen.

When it comes to patience, it's about which choice you want to make and when. It's like taking just enough action to stay afloat, but not splashing away too much so as to go in the wrong direction.

So rather than saying you are or aren't a patient person, a better question would be: in how many situations are you able to practice patience and for how long are you able to endure? Words can shape your mindset in various cases.

Throughout your journey, you're bound to run into situations that will test your patience to its most extreme and fragile limits. Naturally, you'll react in your own unique way depending on the situation you find yourself in.

For example, someone may be exceptionally good at working with children, the elderly or even people with disabilities while others may not be as adept; causing them to throw in the towel much sooner.

No matter the situation, let's begin by eliminating the stigma surrounding losing one's patience in any given circumstance. While it's not the ideal choice in most cases, it doesn't mean that it's wrong.
At worst, losing your patience when you've just about had it with someone or something can be a tad problematic.

At best, it gives the other person a clear signal that they've overstepped your boundaries. Maybe not as efficient, but still effective.

It's important to make the distinction that slipping and falling while you're expanding your boundaries doesn't make you a terrible human being, it makes you human.

Using your underdeveloped abilities as an excuse to cause deliberate harm to others is what makes you a terrible human being.

Your willingness to identify your limits and growing from them, minimizing the amount of times you're failing, is what sets you apart from the terrible crowd.

To achieve this, you must get absolutely clear about what patience means to you and not confuse it with how the world surrounding you defines it.

This isn't an invitation to completely close yourself off to outside advice. That would be like saying put this book down and forget about it. My point is that you want to develop your own personal foundation as to what patience signifies. This will act as your barometer when you're examining other people's perspectives and be able to take them with a grain of salt. Yes, even this one.

When I spoke about this perspective with others, we were able to list how they would define patience in their own terms. The majority of the groups I worked with correlated patience with tolerance.

Meaning that to them patience mostly applies in situations that create stress, discomfort and other negative emotions, or the situations that create unfavorable outcomes.

Examples of this may include being in an argument with someone who isn't seeing eye to eye with you, having to wait extra time at the checkout line of the grocery store, dealing with a child's temper tantrum in an airplane, etc.

Those are very common instances and needless to say there are countless others. However, these are only covering one end of the spectrum.

To round this out far more effectively, you can't fail to acknowledge that patience can be viewed from a stance of positivity as well.

This means being patient when you're doing the things that you enjoy and not just rushing through them. The simple act of slowing down and taking your time, even if you're not engaging in something that is causing you immediate frustration, fear or stress, is also a great exercise to develop your patience.

Take for instance doing tasks that stem from a place of love and tenderness. It could be hobbies such as tending to a garden or painting a large canvas. It could also be something considered laborious, like caring after someone with an illness or trying to explain something to an elderly family member which they may find complex, etc.

In other words, you don't always have to throw yourself against negative events to be able to develop patience. You can look at all the good that's happening around you and practice it just as well, if not better, since you're not in a negative space and you can make clearer choices.

Therefore, patience can be interpreted as a way of measuring your tolerance towards the negative things that you encounter and measuring your flow in life for the positive things you encounter.

This raises the next question in this category and also a very important one.

Where exactly do you draw the line to prevent damage to yourself or others in these situations that push you beyond your threshold?

It's critically important that you identify what you're willing to put up with and for how long. Defining these boundaries early on will significantly boost your progress on improving your patience with yourself and others.

In the next section, you'll be introduced to the two elements that make up patience in this method so that you can define your boundaries and understand yourself and others more thoroughly.

Patience In Practice: Understanding and Compassion

It's important to understand that putting patience into practice doesn't mean you have to allow yourself to be taken advantage of.

It's also important to note that it certainly doesn't mean you have to walk on eggshells around others.

Just as patience doesn't mean total inaction, it doesn't mean total passivity either. The chances of setting yourself up for failure increase astronomically if you buy into the belief that letting others get away with injustice is what patience is about. That's not what it's about.

To begin optimizing your levels of patience, let's further simplify it by breaking it down into two main elements. By getting a grasp of these two, you'll have a much better chance at changing your perspective or reinforcing the one you already may have.

Patience begins with understanding.

To be an understanding person isn't only about having the ability to listen, comprehend and retain a message or feeling being conveyed. I want you to examine understanding in the literal sense of *standing under*.

In other words, by 'standing under' you're using humility to remind yourself that you don't always have to be right in every situation. This is going to be a combination of both patience and courage, however the focus remains on the aforementioned.

When you're trying to understand someone, you're essentially trying to see the reason behind their actions.

To do this effectively, you mustn't perceive what they're saying or doing as a direct attack. This is where things get truly difficult because in a stressful situation, when the pressure is heavier than usual, is when you're more likely to take a defensive stance.

When someone challenges your ideas, opinions, beliefs, or anything else you hold onto dearly, you have to remind yourself that there's a possibility the person you've encountered may be completely misinformed and acting out as a result of misdirection. They may be completely open to learning and might just need you to help them along.

This is in reference to the majority of discussions people have on a daily basis.

For example, trying to reach an agreement at a work meeting or trying to figure out why you may have received the incorrect change after making a purchase.

I'm not referring to an actual threat to your safety. Although not impossible, you don't want to resort to patience if your life or the life of others are in real danger. You'll know more about this in the courage chapter.

Coming back to understanding, to be able to see why someone might be saying or doing the things they're doing, you don't have to dive too deep into their psyche.

You only have to listen openly and validate someone's thoughts and emotions to the best of your abilities. The manner in which someone may express themselves based on their current state of mind is going to make this task either very easy or very difficult for you.

Regardless of what's going on, by understanding where someone is coming from, you give yourself the power you deserve to have by taking the lead and offering to guide someone in their moments of weakness.

It's a bit of a gamble when trying to decipher what's really happening inside someone's mind at any given time, but you're betting alongside the house when you begin with patience under the right climate. This is why no matter what happens, despite what is said or done, the next element to take into consideration is the one that brings it all together.

Compassion is not an easy asset to possess. This is perhaps one of the most important abilities to have, as it lets you feel through and along with the person you're interacting with.

The beauty about compassion is that it isn't completely about you.

This is the stage where you begin to put others before yourself, but it's done at such a level that it supersedes empathy and selflessness.

Why? Remember, patience isn't about inaction.

The real reason is the simple fact that empathy allows you to feel through and along with the person in question. Compassion has both, but also invites the desire to help the other person. That's a distinction worth noting.

Not only that, but compassion also allows you to keep a healthy emotional range between you and anyone or anything else that may prove to be too much to handle.

This is most helpful when you want to remain unbiased in your course of action and reduce the chances of hurting another person despite having their best interest in mind when you choose to help them.

To explain a bit further, one of the best examples I can use here happen to be office spaces.

Now, I'm aware not every one works at an office due to cultural backgrounds, geographical locations, passions, morals and far too many other factors to name in just one book chasing after simplicity. This is why we're going to focus on the most generalized view possible and we'll cover the others in future releases.

For the most part, organizations that you work for will require you to uphold their ideals, their vision, their guidelines and regulations. Unless you're the owner of the business, there's very little wiggle room here to deviate from the established rules.

The downside to this is if you handle difficult situations on your own and you take it upon yourself to take action without guidance or patience, you're more likely to have to answer for them later on if they happen to land you on the hot seat in your boss' office.

For example, giving a co-worker, employee, or a client sufficient time to express a troubling case or feeling is already difficult enough, especially if you're in a management position.

Now imagine throwing company protocol in the mix, limiting what you can do and how you can do it. What happens when other people go against the rules that are predetermined for yourself? This is often the case since other people don't know what rules your work requires you to play by.

With that in mind, it's virtually game over before it even begins. You can't control how other people behave, you can only control your own behavior.

When I investigated cases like these for the industries I've worked with, I've seen how following certain procedures in tough situations has backfired on employees when it's labeled as misconduct, nepotism or even sexual harassment.

In some of these cases, employees who are impacted by the fine print of corporate policies unfortunately will begin to tune out because of the drop in their morale. This of course decreases the efficiency of work.

You may be in a similar situation if you're on autopilot through your work shifts and ultimately getting more disconnected with each passing day.

I can only imagine what kind of burden you might be carrying when you're finally off the clock. We're so caught up in wanting to correct others that we forget that we're mostly wrong ourselves.

What does all of this have to do with patience?

Taking your time and slowing down could be as simple as not rushing to offer solutions when the other person just wants to be heard during a discussion. In the workplace, simply listening to your clients or employees is key.

This isn't just to get a sale or get them to go away, but to help de-escalate potential conflicts and save more time than trying to just prove a point to someone because that's "just company policy."

In other cases not related to work, being patient could mean doing something for a friend or family member that would otherwise be a minor inconvenience or a minor annoyance but their happiness would take precedence.

Take for example, spending a few extra minutes giving your partner a massage, enjoying a sunset together, or it could even be as simple as being present with someone you care for and not necessarily interact with them. Just listening, just being there.

Your body is full of energy. Being there, in the moment, can be so priceless for others.

On that aspect, personal relationships are a tad more complicated than professional ones when it comes to practicing patience. Mainly because work isn't something that typically follows you home most of the time, whereas you're spending every other waking moment with your partner if you're already locked into a relationship or even married.

Another reason why personal relationships are trickier is because the challenges that you encounter obviously won't play by the same rules.

For example, if you don't like something in particular at work, the guidelines and rules in place make it very easy to solve the problems you face. You have the support and guidance of staff and colleagues. This help is often very straightforward and diplomatic, calling for little effort from your part.

For personal relationships, there is no staff. No rule book. Little to no input from outside influences.

In most cases, personal relationships can turn from blissful into a free-for-all very quickly.

One of the more obvious times when you may want to exercise patience is when an argument or disagreement takes place between you and your significant other. This can also apply to arguments with friends. The source of the argument is not really too important, though it can definitely contribute to just how quickly things can escalate.

Issues such as budgeting, the children and even the way the laundry is folded can create some very interesting discussions between people.

Jealousy, lack of communication, and other types of fall-outs can pile on to just about any other argument you have with someone you're interacting with.

Once again, the root of the problem isn't too important because the solution is one-size fits all.

What's really important to note is how the feelings and thoughts are being expressed, how frequent they happen to be, how long they're lasting each time and seeking middle ground in ways that satisfy both people involved.

Unfortunately, it's not always as easy as that. Since emotions are engaged in different ways at home than they are at work, knowing that love and affection can sometimes devolve into obsession and manipulation makes applying patience during these types of disagreements a formidable challenge.

Remember though, that patience isn't always about dealing with the negative. It can come in the form of doing things to please someone other than yourself.

An example of this can be devoting your personal time to prepare a surprise for your significant other while they're at work or making plans with friends or family who you haven't seen in a while.

Inversely, your significant other could also apply the same skill and be more compassionate with their choices. There should be mutual effort in understanding each other and asking the right questions to level the playing field. After all, when it comes to personal relationships, it's all about the team effort.

Even when it's not someone you're romantically involved with, by applying this practice with friends, family or even other people who share a common goal or interest, you'll notice how much smoother situations can flow when compassion is placed at the forefront and shared openly.

Achieving all of these things can take time and that's the key here. Not many people have the ability to give what you're looking for at the exact moment you ask for it. This is why you shouldn't set your expectations so high at the beginning of any engagement.

Through calm examination and thoughtfulness by means of compassion and understanding, the vast majority of your personal and professional relationships should not suffer as much.

There are countless of other challenges unique to personal relationships, each with their own constraints and setbacks.

It's important to not react impulsively causing you to turn against one another, or even begrudging the other person for doing something in a manner you're not used to.

Keeping an open mind and an open heart is the key to patience. Lead by example and show others what can be achieved with a little bit of time well spent in observation before taking any kind of action.

You and only you are in control of how you convey your thoughts and emotions. It's as easy as stopping and listening.

This brings us to looking at yourself and your own actions.

Even though there will be times when despite not being directly involved with a business or another human being, you still may end up being a little too hard on yourself.

As the saying goes, you are your own worst enemy.

Briefly explained, you can be more patient with yourself when you experience loss or failure by allowing yourself to make mistakes as part of your learning process.

You may also use patience as a way to organize your daily tasks more effectively, so that you're not rushing from one place to the next.

It's self-evident that patience pays off in various situations involving direct and indirect interactions. You may be asking what happens when patience runs out. I've met several people who are devoted to spiritual practices which allow them to display impressive levels of compassion and understanding.

For many others who don't follow such practices or anything else to keep them grounded, it's a matter of time before something tests their limits.

Life isn't meant to be easy by any means.

Some people and situations won't allow you to slow down and process things more effectively. This doesn't mean that it can't be as simple as you need it to be. In case you find yourself struggling, I can tell you that the difficult times are the best times to take a step back and re-examine what patience means to you once again.

To give you an idea, at one point in my life I wasn't too fond of public speaking.

This meant anything dealing with work presentations, hosting meetings with employees, speaking in large groups or parties or even conducting interviews about my books and projects.

In my line of work at that time, I knew that learning to engage with large audiences would bring me incredible rewards and earn me more respect than simply sending out mass emails or having a phone conference where people wouldn't be able to put a face to the name.

One of the greater obstacles I battled with while dealing with this insecurity was that I would often rush my speech.

This caused me to stumble over my words or have people ask me to repeat myself after every other thing I said.

Making matters much more challenging, most people I engaged with didn't give themselves enough time to offer any assistance, and instead made things worse with their inability to pause for me.

I still didn't allow this wall in front of me to stop me. In fact, it made me want to spend a greater deal of time learning better communication skills. I took it upon myself to learn a new word every single day and try to use it in a conversation. More importantly, I learned how to slow down my interactions with crowds and individuals, focusing on clarity rather than speed.

Measure twice; cut once.

What I discovered after making this a daily habit was that many people are so caught up in getting their voice to be heard that they forget to stop, listen and think.

This is precisely what leads to miscommunication and it's next to fatal when it comes to any kind of human interaction.

Keep in mind that even by slowing down, listening actively and thinking clearly before speaking, there will still be times that you'll fail. Whenever this happens, be sure to remember that having patience with yourself to learn and fully understand this isn't going to be an overnight process. Mastery will take time, consistency and discipline.

With time and practice, you'll learn to place your focus on the solutions to many problems without losing your own temper despite other people around you struggling to gather themselves. Thoughts and emotions will eventually be processed more smoothly, hence you'll make less reckless decisions.

Most importantly, you'll eliminate a large portion of unwarranted anxiety from your life by seeing that you don't have to worry about as many things as you once thought you did. Many things in life are very trivial, you're the only one responsible for giving them the weight that they have.

I'm not trying to discount the fact that you should stand up for some things from time to time. It's absolutely important to have something worth fighting for. Likewise, that's the weight you're willing to carry, should you choose to.

You'll learn more about this and what is the fuel behind your fire later on.

Mastering Patience

Mastering anything in life is always easier said than done. The first step in order to achieve mastery over patience and consequently everything else will be to become comfortable in the uncomfortable.

This means that when you're presented with an opportunity to expand your levels of compassion and understanding, I encourage you to take it. Despite the pain and the initial confusion of it all, this is a chance worth taking. Make sure you uphold the boundaries you've defined and that they're in line with your natural character; not something that other people determined for you.

Although these questions are unique to me, the point I'm trying to illustrate is that you need to ask yourself the right questions based on your unique path as well.

◆ What's the situation and who is involved? (e.g. is this situation positive or negative? Are you going through this by yourself or are you with others?)

◆ What are some of the things you won't tolerate? (e.g. verbal abuse, being interrupted, being lied to, etc.)

- What are some of the things you won't resort to when facing chaos? (e.g. physical retaliation, substance abuse, isolation, etc.)

- What are the risks and rewards of taking action? (What would be the outcome of taking action versus not taking any action whatsoever?)

- Is exercising patience the best solution for the particular situation you find yourself in? (Is anyone in immediate danger? Are there time constraints in place?)

As mentioned previously, each case will be very different. The things to consider will be limitations of time, number of people impacted, the risk to reward ratio, etc. The idea is to maintain a clear mind as much as possible to be able to expand your levels of patience and keep panic at bay.

In summary, by putting patience at the forefront of your approach to daily life you'll find how much more rewarding everything will be. This goes for both positive and negative situations and tasks.

By making this the primary stepping stone of your journey, you'll notice how the other values you'll learn more about in just a moment will easily fall into place.

Patience Takeaways

◆ **Try to see all challenges, pressures and limitations as opportunities to grow.** They don't necessarily have to be happening to you personally. You can use the events that others go through as your platform to grow as well. Practicing your situational awareness also takes extreme patience, so this can be a great exercise to implement.

◆ **Give equal weight to the exchange of time between you and another person.** This will allow you to give time a greater value from a point of gifting it; not something that is being stolen from you. Time is only as valuable as how you decide to allocate it.

◆ **When people around you make mistakes or things don't go the way you expected them to go, remind yourself to see things from the opposite perspective.** This will help you make more sound decisions and not always resort to being defensive or take offense for things that may be inconsequential or just simple miscommunications.

◆ **Through patience, the choices you make will remain true to your core mission and purpose in this life.** Your path will be less likely to be poorly influenced by other people's inability to control themselves amid chaos. Stay the course and retain your power to change direction should you need to.

If you have the luxury to think things through before moving forward, do it.

◆ **See the imperfections of the world around you with a softer heart and a clearer vision.** This will lead you to be more compassionate and understanding. You also won't be forcing yourself to carry the burdens of others if you give them no weight when it's adequate.

◆ **Practice patience willfully to keep yourself grounded when problems do arise.** Remind yourself to listen actively before speaking, asking the right the questions and seeing things from all angles as much as possible. Not every challenge you face requires you to join.

◆ **Patience isn't limited to putting up with the negative**. You can be patient when things are going well and enjoy the journey itself as much as the prospect of reaching the destination.

◆ **Challenge yourself to seek no instant gratification**. Build your character in such a way that it can't be bribed with the idea of temporary satisfactions, short-term rewards and other vices. This resilience will aid you when the journey eventually becomes long and arduous. This is the apex of mastery over patience.

Now that you have an idea of how to identify the ground you stand on and are able to process what's happening in any situations with more clarity, this allows us to move on to the next section.

Here's where you'll learn to actually mold your mindset to the world around you.

II: Gratitude

"When you arise in the morning, think of what precious privilege it is to be alive. To breathe, to think, to enjoy, to love."

~Marcus Aurelius

We've touched base on the benefits of taking your time to assess the world around you, valuing the time that you exchange with others and taking every opportunity that you can to come from a place of compassion and understanding.

Now, when you're taking every step necessary to make sure you're in the best position possible, it doesn't mean that everything is going to go your way. Things can and will go wrong. This is normal, but there is something I'd like for you to consider and it is the following.

When things do go wrong, you may be saying or doing things that are placing you on the wrong side of the argument without your realization.

One of them happens to be so commonplace that it has become almost expected in many cultures worldwide. It may be something you think nothing of since it's part of your everyday vocabulary or perhaps something that you or other people have noticed since it's used in excess.

Whatever the case may be, I'd like to begin this chapter by declaring something you probably may not agree with.

Stop Apologizing By Default.

Before you rip this book in half, hear me out.

I don't mean you should stop apologizing in the sense that you shouldn't feel remorseful when you cause harm to someone or when you add more unnecessary chaos to a world that needs less of it.

To elaborate further, if someone expressly tells you that you're the reason for their pain, you absolutely should consider offering a sincere apology if you feel it's warranted.

What I really mean by this is you should stop apologizing for things outside of your immediate control and stop approaching things from the angle that you're already in the wrong before you even begin to speak.

Instead, you should be shifting your focus towards expressing gratitude for what you're given rather than what's being taken away.

The purpose behind this is to reprogram your mind to be thankful towards an act or event instead of feeling 'sorry' for it.

Let's dissect this.

I mentioned that you'll run into situations which will test the limits of your patience. Supposing you've already run out of that resource, another one of the more daunting challenges is when you're interacting with someone who isn't too fond of seeing the glass as half-full, is in a low-vibration state or is simply spiritually lost.

Now, experiencing negative emotions or taking a pessimistic stance both have their perks.

Just like anything else, they too have their proper time and place.

For example, imagine how awkward it would be to exercise what I'm sharing in this chapter by expressing gratitude at a funeral... Probably not the best of settings.

By looking at things negatively from time to time, we can identify the positive, because you can't have one without the other. The existence of good implies the existence of evil and vice versa. So, I don't want to completely take away all credit from experiencing those negative sensations, granted they're under your control.

Ultimately, the goal of gratitude here is completely different.

What you want to aim for is to rewire your mind by getting rid of "default pessimism" and turn it into "default optimism". I believe that with a few slight adjustments to your vocabulary and your perspective, the world around you won't seem so dark and so heavy.

To achieve this, of course, you have to begin by identifying what are the things you are grateful for. Additionally, you must know what brings about discomfort so as to know how to see the best that comes along with it.

The things you're grateful for can be as large as the sky above or as subtle as the spoon you stir your cup of tea with.

Likewise, you can be thankful for a disaster you experienced which brought forth the strength you didn't realize you had or taught you something about someone to help you let them go.

Defining Gratitude

What does gratitude mean to you?

When asking this question, what you're really looking for are ways of expression. Many people will agree that a simple 'thank you' is enough to display gratitude towards someone. Others may express it through different means, such as different love languages, their respective archetypes or a combination of these and other ways. There is a wealth of information on those subjects that I won't be covering here, but I encourage you to look into them if you're interested in diving deeper as to why people make the choices they do.

Getting back on track, ask yourself in what ways do you accept someone's gratitude? There are several options available. Is 'thank you' enough? Do you look for grand displays? Or maybe you don't need anything at all to be grateful?

It's important to ask these questions because you need to identify what you're willing to take and willing to give in as many situations as possible.

To give you a better idea, there was a time when I wasn't the best at accepting gifts from others. Even if it was a special occasion such as a birthday or a gift exchange, I never really knew what to make of receiving anything as small as a card or a compliment. It's something I worked on for several years along with my speech.

This is when I begun paying closer attention to how people opened themselves to receiving things, how their expectations were predetermined, how they expressed their gratitude in comparison to mine, etc.

Another end of the spectrum here is to ensure that you're apologizing for things that are actually under your control.

This is the kind of mindset you want to be setting yourself up for day in and day out. To do this, you'll want to consider the following elements that make up gratitude in this method.

Gratitude In Practice: Sincerity and Adaptability

You wouldn't apologize for the weather, would you? So why should it be any different for anything else you don't control?

I question this because you don't want to remain under the veil of assuming wrongdoing before the event or reaction takes place.

In order to change this mindset, your focus should be to turn the negatives into positives in all major areas of your daily life.

I want to reiterate that apologizing isn't wrong.

What you want to try and do is remind yourself to begin and end things on positive notes whenever you can.

First of all, in order to effectively employ gratitude, you must consider sincerity.

If you don't mean what you say and it doesn't fall in line with your core values, don't say it. Of course, this is better applied for serious actions and not ones done in jest, although you must tread carefully there as well.

Besides watering the weight of apologies down to common gestures that are spoken any time something mildly inconvenient happens, (e.g. asking someone to let you pass through a narrow space) you're inadvertently training yourself to approach situations from a place of undesired submission. Not to mention, you're teaching others to treat you in accordance with how you present yourself.

Meaning, if you're instantly assuming the guilt, then guess who they're more likely to blame if it comes down to it.

Florence Scovel Shinn, an artist and author of 1900's fame, spoke of the infinite spirit and of the existence of a supply for every demand. In other words, she spoke of God and his limitless wisdom. The way I see this, if you supply someone with a sense of submission, the demand will become one of negativity and blame. Inversely, if you control the supply through gratitude, the demand will become one of positivity and not guilt.

If you understand the power behind your self-expression and what you ask God for, you'll understand that you're able to manifest many things in your life through His grace. Hence, you mustn't assume guilt prematurely unless you truly are responsible for something gone wrong.

Taking this a step further, let's suppose you're sincerely concerned that you may be inconveniencing someone you're approaching. Maybe they were busy with some other task or you didn't want to appear disrespectful by assuming you're on friendly terms.

If that happens to be the case, and you automatically present yourself with an apology, consider ending the conversation with positive reinforcement and gratitude. It seems obvious, but it's something you may often forget to do.

Even if you do inconvenience someone, reminding them of the good they did for you instead of placing your focus on the way you inconvenienced them will warrant a better response from the interaction.

It's more difficult for someone to willfully turn down a grateful expression, especially when it's one backed by sincerity. Like any apology, the expression of gratitude should fall in accordance with the overall experience.

I doubt you'll want to express thanks to someone who is rude to you or is attacking you for no given reason or apologize to someone who isn't blaming you to begin with.

"Sorry" can lose its value just like any other phrase that's used too often. You run the risk of cheapening it and taking its power away after so many uses in situations that don't require it.

I mentioned in the patience chapter that conflict is inevitable. When patience runs low, and it will, adaptability is another element of gratitude that you must consider.

Why? Because not everything that happens to you or everyone you meet is out to destroy you.

"Thank you" is also a phrase that can be worn out. The question is, if you had to use one of the two, it's better to be thankful, right? Why must you apologize if you've done nothing wrong?

There are better ways of expressing your thoughts and feelings without being so apologetic by default.

With this said, attempting to take a grateful stance in many cases will help you learn more about the world around you by taking it for what it is and not what you think it should be. This is how you can adapt to situations, molding them to your will and granting you more power over chaos.

Not to mention you're not going to burden yourself by carrying unnecessary weights, in reference to what other people or the world itself decides to dump on you. Unless you plan on using it for your own development, you don't need to stress yourself out beyond your capabilities. This is about giving permission for things and people to affect you. It's a daunting challenge, but one that makes you more flexible and adaptable to the unpredictability of events happening around you.

There are various tactics you can use to not perceive events as damaging. To see the silver lining you'll have to come from a place of understanding and combine that with a sense of gratitude. In essence, you can level the playing the field by not giving your power away when things happen to be going against you.

Make it daily challenge to turn the negatives into positives. Remember, this isn't to say you should have complete disregard for someone's sincere sense of grief, anger, or confusion when they're going through a challenge of their own.

What you're doing here is using a mixture of validation, compassion and understanding to tackle the issue rather than instinctively defend yourself against it, as if it were some sort of attack. With this effort, you'll be able to see the benefits as they reveal themselves and practice gratitude more efficiently.

First, you must carefully and thoroughly assess the situation you find yourself in. Remember, be patient. It'll take time and plenty of practice until the following process gets easier each time.

◆ **Is the situation something that is under your direct control?** (e.g. burned out light bulb, argument with your spouse, disagreement with a close friend, etc.)

- **Is it something that can be solved with the help of an established set of rules?** (e.g. company policies, local laws, instruction manual, etc.)

- **If it can't be solved with the established set of rules, what are the alternative solutions?** (In other words, what are some exceptions to the rules that can be made to reach a solution?)

- **How severe will the impact be if this situation isn't taken care of?**
  (e.g. will people lose their job, will your relationships come to an end, will money be lost, is someone's health at stake, etc.)

These questions will yield you clearer answers, thus eliminating unnecessary worry and stress. Focus on how the problem will be solved and be thankful for the wisdom you gained to reach this conclusion. It's a shift in perspective that will be far more beneficial to you rather than dwelling on the things that went wrong, or worse, assuming guilt for them ahead of time.

Mastering Gratitude

If we're continuously misled to believe that most of the things we say or do are automatically wrong, we're more likely to shut down in social situations that need bold input.

I've outlined these examples to give you a better idea of where your perspective should be when disaster strikes. In all reality, however, there are no right or wrong answers here. Everyone's experience will be unique.

For the gratitude mastery chapter, I'll highlight the example of romantic relationships, since these present far greater challenges than you can find in professional or platonic ones.

For instance, disagreements like deciding what to make for dinner, who's turn is it to feed the baby or why you didn't take out the trash after your partner asked you to.

Personally, I find gratitude in relationships to be one of my favorite areas to discuss.

You may know people who are often so preoccupied with being correct all the time that they forget that through compassion, understanding and gratitude, a ton of problems can be neutralized if not avoided altogether.

If you're ever responsible for issuing a sincere apology for something, remind yourself to be just as sincerely grateful for the lessons learned, moving forward and not dwelling on the past. The best apology is in fact changed behavior.

If you wish to change any troublesome behavior, you must be receptive to change and cheerful for its positive influence as opposed to fighting against it.

In matters of the heart, you can be thankful for the things your partner does for you.

If you're in a stable relationship, it's no secret that appreciating the little things goes a long way.

This may be acts of kindness, quality time spent together, respecting your personal time away from them, or not gawking at other people who may be more physically attractive.

Still, it's very important that you pay closer attention to all of the times that you're apologizing for things that you are unable to control. This is one of the many ways that you can begin training your mind to start spotting the benefits of certain situations when the majority of people are only focused on what's going wrong and what could only get worse.

This is why the use of positive reinforcement is helpful. The primary focus will be to acknowledge if the problem was under your control, be thankful if you're able to correct it and keeping your eyes focused on the solution.

Using positive reinforcement allows you to highlight the positive attributes of others and yourself in times of chaos, instead of using energy in a wasteful manner by directing it towards the source of pain, suffering and discomfort.

A classic example of this comes from the service industry. "Sorry for the wait" is much better applied as "thank you for your patience."

If you're in an argument with someone, as long as you remain patient, you're able to highlight their ability to express themselves sincerely and openly, instead of trying to turn it into a contest and "winning". You would be surprised how much you could learn from others by simply pausing for a moment and listening.

When you make an effort to leave things on a positive note, you will greatly reduce any feelings of guilt and resentment that the person apologizing may develop otherwise. It will also help you be more open to solutions presented from different perspectives instead of punishing one another over things that are more than likely already solved.

Finally, being grateful with yourself is the most rewarding of all steps. You're likely to take things for granted every now and then and, this too, is normal.

For example, things like the roof over your head, your job, your friend circles, or even romantic partners. Sooner or later, you may lose these due to unforeseen circumstances or even your own negligence. Life is already supremely volatile and mostly unpredictable, so to exercise gratitude in both the good and the bad is going to put you leagues ahead of the game.

Everything that happens in your lifetime is there to teach you something about yourself. You can't punish yourself if you fail to understand the lessons right away. The answers don't always present themselves at the moment you wish to have them.

If you can begin to see things happening for you instead of to you, you'll gain an outstanding advantage in your journey.

Lastly, take a good look in the mirror sometime and ask yourself what did you accomplish today? Did you make your bed? Take out the garbage?

Landed that bonus at work? What about the things you didn't get to do? Maybe you had to cancel an important interview or reschedule a lunch outing with a friend? Will you have time to get these things done in the next day or two?

Think of all the challenges you put yourself through, big or small. There are some people who don't feel accomplished after completing their entire to-do list, while others are just grateful to be up and out of bed; moving and breathing.

If you struggle with this as well, consider picking two or three must-do daily tasks and appreciate the chance you have to complete them or even just to attempt them.

It's easy to be grateful for the good things such as being in good health, good spirits, having a book to read or getting any small task done. You can't leave the inconveniences out either.

For example, if you consider washing the dishes to be problematic, I would say try to cherish it appropriately and often. Many people don't have dishes to clean, let alone food to eat.

So to complain about even the smallest of things isn't something you want to make a habit. Nonetheless, gratitude towards the things that many consider minor grievances and gratitude for all that you achieve doesn't have to be a grand, ceremonial display either. A simple, silent thought in the comfort of your own soul will suffice.

Incorporating gratitude into your daily routine will lead you to achieve greater things by redirecting your focus away from all the things that cause unneeded stress. You may be surprised to find how many of these things are virtually sucking your time and energy away like vampires.

Even if something or someone impacts you in an unexpected way, taking a toll along with them, you'll be able to identify what's truly under your direct control in any scenario and make conscious choices more easily. This is how you can begin reinterpreting the unfairness of life as more of a gift each passing day.

Another common way to express gratitude is if you're a believer of a particular religion or a follower of a spiritual practice. This isn't to say that you're incapable of being grateful if you're someone who is atheist or something else of sort.

It's simply easier to illustrate the example of gratitude when you have a set of preexisting rules or guidelines for the body and soul which you abide by.

In contrast, even if you're not a devout believer of any deities or powers beyond the flesh, your path towards appreciation for experiences in life are still just as valid regardless of the incorporation of religious and spiritual texts or practices.

Despite the way of expression being clearly different for different types of people, the one thing that you can use to facilitate the journey is the belief in something greater than yourself. Whether that's a god, the universe itself, the roles that archetypes play in people, magic, an organization with a mission that you support or whatever else you wish to grant that power to.

This could even apply to yourself, although it may prove to be a little tricky to use autotheism to benefit others if you find yourself at the peak of the mountain.

Showing gratitude for what you currently have is also another excellent way of developing an abundance mindset as opposed to one of scarcity.

Wanting more out of life isn't wrong in itself, it's the act of ceaseless wanting that makes things troublesome.

I'm referring specifically to wanting the material or the unnecessary.

If you want the fancy beach house and the bank account with multiple commas, that's great. So long as these material desires don't completely consume you and blind you to what's really necessary.

You must know when enough is enough for yourself, your family and your community.

When greed and selfishness grab hold of you, it's difficult to break free from them until you face the consequences of each. You can work yourself to death trying to amass material fortunes, only to miss out on important experiences with loved ones or even in peaceful solitude, if your hunger for the material and the unnecessary is insatiable.

This is where you should take into consideration what you deem unnecessary. We all have different necessities; some more than others. But when you think of the basics, how much do you truly need versus how much do you want?

Well, you can begin by asking yourself what you really want. Why do you want it or need it? What makes you believe you don't already have it?

Obviously, if what you want at this time is a boat because you want to explore the oceans and it's not waiting for you at the pier already, then that answers most of the questions. Maybe you're an intrepid sailor or fisherman waiting to discover the open waters, therefore you need the right equipment for that. If that happens to be the case, then excellent.

You can use this boat to your benefit and the benefit of those around you if that's all you need to begin your journey at sea.

Especially if it's something you truly love therefore it won't feel like you're doing any real work by chasing after it.

We can look deeper into this by saying you only want a boat for leisure and not to make a living for yourself. That's fine also, this could be your way of coping with stress. Maybe you want it to take trips alone or with loved ones at will; escaping the harsh realities of daily life. That's also beneficial in its own way.

Now, one reason is obviously more practical than the other. You wouldn't want to spend your life savings on a fleet of boats unless you're looking to turn them into a fishing fleet or rent them to other seafarers. This is why wanting something just because you want it can be dangerous.

In reference to virtues and values, such as gratitude in this case, it's not about what you lack but what you have. Maybe you want ten boats but can only afford one at any given time. As long as your expectations are not too exorbitant, one boat can bring you as much joy as ten, granted you use it properly and take care of it to aid you in whatever it is that you seek.

Maintaining realistic expectations reduces and eliminates any disillusion when you don't get what you want.

This is how you learn to place value on the things that matter and other people despite their flaws.

Sure, you may not have as many boats as your neighbor, but true wealth and happiness can be attained by simply taking a look around, taking a look inward or just not looking at all and letting things be as they are.

Gratitude Takeaways

Even though it may not be apparent at first, introducing positive reinforcement in a sincere way when you don't get your way does you and others a great favor. This also aids you with your adaptability, which is why the gratitude pattern is as simple as all the rest.

I'm not suggesting the impossible which is for you to be positive about everything all the time, for that is just as ineffective as being negative all the time.

There will be days that will test your strength, forcing you to go through the motions of chaos. Experiencing negative thoughts, feelings and tumultuous events are not ideal, but they will help you get the most out of your limited life experience.

The idea here is that through gratitude, the weights of life will become lighter and the silver lining in situations that arise unexpectedly will become more vivid. You have far more control than you give yourself credit for.

By developing your sense of gratitude, you give yourself the power to mold the world around you, unnecessary wanting will become suppressed and you'll begin to value even what others consider disastrous from their perspective.

The keys to remember are as follows.

◆ **Acknowledge the situation for what it is.** Don't assume instant fault or guilt for a problem unless you're directly involved in its cause.
   If you must assume responsibility for your actions, include positive reinforcement in your approach so as to train your mind to see the value in these lessons; not their inconvenience.

◆ **If a problem has been identified, focus on the solution.** You can spend hours discussing what can go wrong. Why not use that same energy to discuss what has gone right or what can go right? Redirect your focus.

◆ **Be grateful for the lessons learned and the experience gained.** Consider expressing gratitude instead of automatically resorting to apologies. Once again, this isn't meant to be taken as having complete disregard for someone's grief or pain, especially if you caused it. This is about being content with the knowledge you gained to overcome a problem if it happens. Even if no immediate solution was found, rest easy knowing that all chaos eventually subsides and the good will show itself soon.

◆ **Wealth is derived from finding value in what you have, not what you lack.** If you're constantly wanting, you'll always be empty. If you love what you have, you'll notice it's plenty. Whatever you seek in life, be mindful of your limits, what falls under necessities and what falls under mere wants. Take only what you need, make do with what you have and be thankful of what you're given by others, by the universe and by God.

◆ **Take the perspective of things happening for you rather than to you. This is how you can overcome mostly anything in life.** Things happen for a reason and a purpose. Despite these answers not being clear or making complete sense, remember that it's okay. Through patience, the truth will always reveal itself. Through gratitude, this truth can be beneficial, not harmful. This means less finger-pointing and more thoughtful assignation of responsibility.

◆ **Make a habit of thanking your shortcomings often.**
This may seem contradicting but it's good to give
credit where credit is due, even to the things that
inconvenienced you. It's a matter of rewiring your
mind to be accepting rather than inflexible. How do
you know you can change a flat tire if you never have
to deal with one? It's during your weakest moments
that you realize how strong you truly are. By seeing
this angle, you'll gain your power back and are no
longer a victim of circumstance or your surroundings.

On that last point, we enter the final value worth its own
weight in gold. Primarily because it calls for strong, direct
action in the majority of cases where time and optimism
aren't on your side.

III: Courage

*"In order to change, you sometimes must wage war on
yourself. You must be merciless with your demons and be
absolutely fearless when turning the pages of the book
written by the better you."*

Courage becomes paramount when patience fails, when
gratitude is non-existent, when you're at your wits end and
the world turns into a certain kind of monster towards you.
Courage can be defined in several ways, but it's much

easier to pinpoint when things are genuinely out to hurt you and you're forced to strike back twice as hard.

Life is difficult enough as is and we don't make it any easier for one another sometimes.

Though most people seek to live in harmony, there are those who truly just wish to watch the world burn. You'll run into people who won't abide by any rules or standards set by the communities they live in. This can happen by conscious choice or be due to some terrible misfortune, such as a mental incapability to remain structured.

Other misfortunes such as accidents, natural disasters and unexpected illness can line up in such a way that can leave you vulnerable to your own demons and the other demons that roam the earth freely.

When I say "demons", I'm referring to the forces that are outside of your control; not the literal demons of tales and scripture.

These demons will make it far too easy for you to consume yourself with stress and pessimism when you're caught between the sword and a hard place.

Regardless of how circumstances are shaped beyond your control or how many literal demons you happen to be fighting at any given time, the truth is this can either make

you or destroy you. Hence, the way to close the gap
through courage begins with this statement:

Stop Being Harmless.

Clinical psychologist Dr. Jordan B. Peterson has done great
work for the community with his powerful stances across a
multitude of topics. Of the many things he speaks about,
there's one that I believe is one of his most profound ideas.

It is that you must unleash the monster inside of you and
then you should learn to control this monster.

For me, it's virtually an untouchable statement and one
that I agree with wholeheartedly. To elaborate a bit more,
despite attaining mastery over patience and gratitude,
there will be situations that call for immediate action and
may also require you to be dangerous but disciplined.

Many members of the spiritual communities may attribute
this to a segment of "shadow work".

Now, that's not to say you should go out in the street and
start beating your chest in hopes of getting your way
through nothing but aggression; proving the rest of this
book pointless.

Let's interpret this correctly.

The challenge for you in darker times, especially with seemingly boundless political strife, social conflict, police brutality and other chaotic events is to always try to resort to patience first. You must take it upon yourself to find and feel the ground you stand on before taking unnecessary risks. This will often prove more useful for you than trying to power your way through arguments or clashes of any other type.

However, there will be times when your steel will be tested. If you're able to understand what's happening and can predict the outcome, you can then make a more conscious choice to show dominance and call upon your integrated shadow only when it's truly needed.

Not for the sole purpose of causing harm or destruction, but to guide yourself and others through chaos fearlessly and making difficult decisions quickly and efficiently.

Defining Courage

What does courage mean to you?

Do you identify courage as a lack of fear or acknowledging fear and taking action regardless? Does courage come in the form of taking no action whatsoever under pressure? Do you consider escaping an act of courage?

There are several ways of interpreting this and just like all the other values, you must learn which one of these interpretations makes sense to your unique path. This way, the choices you make remain true to who you identify with.

Psychiatrist and psychoanalyst Carl Jung is another outstanding influence when speaking about the value of courage and the philosophy of the integrated shadow. He goes into great detail about how the shadow is something we must confront openly for us to integrate and tame instead of repressing it. There's a wealth of content about this subject available out there if you want to explore further.

For the purpose of simplicity, I won't be deviating too much from the main topic which is to break down, understand and ultimately gain mastery over courage.

When you define courage, an easy example is to think of the hero defeating the evil foe after a long and difficult battle.

The world is crawling with so many potential enemies, there might be a full catalog somewhere for you to choose one or two from. For me, one of the best ways I want you to understand how you can develop courage is by recognizing the greatest war that not many people dare to speak of.

The war against yourself.

Carl Jung wrote: "No tree, it is said, can grow to heaven without its roots reaching down to hell." I'm going to use this quote to help guide you through the development of courage in your day to day life with the use of the shadows within yourself.

Courage In Practice: Passion and Consequence

You can look at courage as facing your fears, overcoming adversity or even choosing to stand down in the face of conflict. Since it's a war we're talking about, there are two key elements that make up courage so you can gain a better understanding of how you can develop it.

Passion is supremely important in any aspect of life, especially in war. For what good is a fight if you don't know why you're fighting to begin with?

Maybe brutes and savages will disagree with me there, but there aren't many of those in the modern world to be concerned with.

Simply put, without passion, there won't be meaningful direction or adequate propulsion. It doesn't mean you're not courageous, it just makes the journey more difficult than it needs to be. Think of it like this: if courage is the vehicle, passion is the ignition. It's the burning flame that lights the path of any journey you embark on.

This is precisely why it's critical for you to identify what you're passionate about before you engage in any sort of bravery test. This is easy for some, difficult for others and nearly impossible for a few.

To help you along in identifying your passion, ask yourself some of the following questions.

◆ **What are some hobbies or things you can always come back to if money wasn't an object?** In other words, where would your heart lead you if you had nothing to lose? (e.g. do you enjoy cooking, doing research, botany, swimming, etc.)

◆ **Is the hobby or thing you're passionate about profitable and helpful?** Is what you're willing to fight for beneficial to you, your family and your community? If not, why not and can that change?

◆ **If you can't think of anything you're passionate about, can you think about things that you aren't passionate about?** Maybe you can't think of what you like. What about your dislikes? Through this process of elimination, you're guaranteed to find something you can live for.

Remember the reason you need to have passion is to have a sense of direction. To be extra clear, I'm not equating aimlessness with unhappiness. I know several nomads who find bliss in the thrill of not knowing where life will take them. It doesn't mean they're lost in life. Or who knows, maybe they are. Does that mean they're unhappy or unfulfilled? Not necessarily.

What I know for sure is that it's a little funny that they find passion in having "no passions". That's a different topic for a different book.

Along with the right sense of direction, passion provides powerful meaning to your journey. It's the reason why you chose to go in the direction you're headed and why you plan on seeing things through to the end. Hence, your passion should be something of an explosive force. Like the thrust it takes to lift a rocket off the ground and shoot out to space.

Something else that you must acknowledge is that passion is an extreme realm to step into. This means that you could end up loving something or someone so obsessively that it becomes detrimental to you and others.

Far worse, you can fall in love with chaos itself from the perspective of perpetuating it.

In either case, remember that chaos isn't something that is inherently evil. You may still find this beneficial if you can use the extreme ends of the spectrum wisely.

For example, if you're the type of person that loves very deeply, instead of channeling this energy to stalk someone or becoming possessive, you could aim to use this loving energy to contribute to the world around you.

This could be something like finding a profession alongside nature, volunteering with animal care services or even looking after the ill and the wounded in a hospital. Examining chaos itself, if that's more to your natural liking, the power you hold is one you must use carefully. Instead of reducing yourself to committing petty crimes, harm or deceive people on purpose, you might make for an excellent member of a demolition crew. Your ability to replace old with the new by understanding explosives, for example, can save companies a lot of money, making you valuable to them.

Or, you could train to become a professional boxer, using your passion to gain knowledge in the art of fighting and making you an outstanding athlete.

Needless to say you want to make sure your passion is towards something that can be profitable, helpful, or both; to you and others. What you don't want to end up doing during your own personal discovery is find yourself directing your passion unwisely, hurting others and yourself in the process.

This is why consequence is the next element of courage. The outcome of the choices you make should help you determine if the path you've chosen is the one to continue on.

Even if you're unable to determine the outcome for a particular choice you're about to make, you still exercise your sense of courage this way by taking action in the face of uncertainty.

You think it would be easy to know the outcome of every single thing you do, but that's not always the case. It's impossible to always know what could happen despite your best intentions and despite the conditions of any situation coming together harmoniously. Anything can happen at any time.

Life is a guessing game and your best guess is your best bet.

Hence, you should start with patience in an ideal scenario. Going through a compassionate and understanding approach, you can expect a similar outcome.

Even with that in mind, a life of pure passivity isn't one in which you can thrive in. This is where gratitude comes in and becomes the middle ground.

It's the bridge connecting two worlds or two people that otherwise would be lost in the valley of miscommunication.

Gratitude is where order and chaos meet, in the sense that you can shape your circumstances to benefit you rather than harm you or cause you unnecessary suffering.
If both of those fail, courage is then necessary to face the uncertainties and the chaos head on. This allows you to own them to the fullest. Here is where things like pushing through fear, anxiety, imminent danger and even surrendering can define you and your path.

Breeding courage is easier than it sounds, even more so than the other core values.

Sooner or later, you'll be exposed to the evil that lies in the hearts of all men and women. This may be something very small to notice, such as a mean glance or a poor attitude. It could also be much greater, like someone deliberately causing you real irreversible harm or even death.

You may have been taught to avoid confrontation as much as possible, especially if you're not geared adequately to handle it appropriately. Confrontation is made up of many layers and comes in many forms to us since we're the ones that give any confrontation its meaning. It can show up in the form of arguments with our coworkers, leading to petty answers such as spreading gossip or harassing one another on a daily basis making the workplace unnecessarily toxic and disorderly.

You could be driving back home and confrontation can show up in the form of someone cutting you off, causing a road rage incident.

Your personal relationships are no exception to this. This could be fights with your spouse over finances or who needs to clean the bathroom, arguments based on miscommunication or jealousy, or even confusion caused over a text message that an old friend sent you in the middle of the night.

As I mentioned before, you'll even confront yourself when you're facing your own darkest thoughts, your uncontrolled vices and repressed negative emotions.

This is the battle that I feel can benefit you the most since no one knows you better than yourself. If you can master yourself, you can master anything.

However, if you're not careful enough with this, it is as risky as it is rewarding. The war with yourself can shred you up and spit you out if you don't channel your dark energies in productive ways.

Beyond yourself, the powers of nature are as chaotic and confrontational as they're beautiful and peaceful.

Oftentimes, nature will tend to test your extremes with sudden, violent weather changes, global disasters such as the pandemic we faced not too long ago or a myriad of other disasters piled on top of each other.

It's through all of these challenges where courage is abundant. Even if you can rid yourself of all other types of conflict, that kind of life wouldn't yield you much.
You wouldn't know strength if not during your moments of weakness. You can't live too cautiously, for these types of risks are sometimes necessary.

Otherwise, when you run into something or someone that clashes with you, it will send you fleeing into a crisis.
Your mind wouldn't be prepared to handle conflict appropriately and that's far more dangerous than taking the risks you needed to before. This is because not only are you in the face of adversity, but you also strip yourself of the control over its outcome.

When Jung said that "no tree can grow to heaven without being rooted in hell", you can look at it from the angle of being able to help yourself experience malevolence through the careful examination of your passions and the consequences associated with them. You must be willing to explore your inner wars, confront your shadows directly by finding their meaning and direction, and live with the consequence of how you address them.

This is how courage is most easily developed and also how your inner wars can be dominated.

You can start this process with your everyday tasks by having a starting point and an end goal; in other words a mission statement. It doesn't have to be a complex mission full of twists and turns, or even one that you have to live out yourself.

To paint an example for you through the lens of the storyteller, let's pretend your mission is as easy as going to the grocery store and making it back home in one piece.

Let's say you and another customer are pulling into the same parking space that's closest to the store.

You both want it and will stop at nothing to get it. After some time, neither of you are budging. You both resort to hand gestures signaling the beginning of a confrontation. Here is a process you can follow to see if courage would be your best option in this situation.

This is often a quick mental process of elimination to assess how successfully you may engage or escape.

◆ **What's the fight really worth to you?** Is it just about a parking space? Is it truly a demonstration of courage, integrity or pride? What else could this possibly mean to someone else, like your family and their safety?

◆ **What would be the consequences of your actions?** What could happen if you get the spot, walk away and the other person is still upset? What would be the consequences of inaction and letting the other person take it?

◆ **What's there to gain or lose?** How much more time could you save by just looking for another spot? Or would you rather just save your wounded ego?

As an alternative, let's assume you've never experienced that type of conflict or don't care to purposely place yourself in those kinds of situations.

If you think that not putting yourself through these types of challenges will hinder you from growing in certain aspects of life, fret not. The solution for that is as simple as looking around you.

By using vicarious experiences to learn something about yourself in such a way that most people may not care to explore, or simply don't know they can, you'll still earn a little more of the wisdom you seek.

You see, peeling back each layer of your reality will reveal how peace and chaos are intertwined in a dance every single passing moment.

Perhaps not as easily visible to the human eye like watching customers of a grocery store argue over a parking spot or having a tug of war over a gallon of milk.

This can be understood in a way that nature is often performing this dance of destruction and creation nearly every second. Even down to a molecular level, cells die and new ones are made without you even realizing it, although that's another subject.

In all, for one thing to exist, its opposite must also exist. You can't have creation without destruction or light without darkness. Meaning that to establish your courage, you must acknowledge and face your fears and insecurities. Whether you do it on your own or live through others to help you along, the result is the same.

This is the reason why a tree must be rooted in hell in order for it to reach heaven.

If you prefer to dissect the experiences around you to gain the knowledge you search for, I wouldn't want you to go down an endless road of 'what if' scenarios. There are too many things to pay attention to at any given moment and scanning all corners of this approach with questions and overthinking is likely to burn your mind out very quickly.

The glaring problem with this is that you'll become trapped in noisy speculation. True, it's helpful in moderation but I'm not here to drive you completely mad with trying to find meaning in things that won't always serve you, so we'll go back to the example of integration of the shadow.

I'd like to reiterate the importance of the tree rooted in hell because you will go through your own unique trials in life.

There's no person that has ever lived a perfect life in the sense of not having to face chaos and other troubles. Even if someone managed to accomplish a life free of all of that, someone is bound to come along and shatter that idea with their unique perspectives and standards. After all, one person's idea of heaven may very well be another person's idea of hell.

The fact remains that all the trials you face in life always come full-circle back to you and you only.
Alas, this is why the hardest battle of your life is the one battle you'll often fight alone and one you'll fight against yourself. It may happen with or without warning. You can be sound asleep in your bed in the middle of the night or it can strike you when you're at a gathering with other people.

No matter where you find yourself, how this battle finds you or when it ambushes you, patiently examine and prepare yourself. Should it reach you at point in life when you're in your prime, be grateful. Lastly, be courageous in your approach to learn the most important lessons that life holds for you by engaging in it.

Mastering Courage

For this chapter, I'm going to share my personal tale of courage with you. If you find yourself in a similar situation, I hope it strikes the right chord for you to take the necessary action in spite of the fear of failure, judgment, abandonment or any other fear you encounter. Now that you're able to better understand your surroundings through patience and mold your perspective through gratitude, through courage is how you'll achieve victory when the other two values don't fall into place as they should.

Earlier on, when speaking about becoming a monster and taming it, I first exposed myself to the chaos of the world around me and the world within me when I joined the military in 2010. Now, I experienced a great deal of chaos when I was much younger too, but the true pivotal moment came when I decided to fight a battle that I thought was much bigger than my own.

It took a while for me to realize the mission I signed up for didn't quite line up with my passions as I hoped it would. To elaborate, I noticed that my purpose to join this fight didn't match the motives of the old men and women calling the shots from the comfort of their offices. To me, their efforts could've been put to better use by aiding the nation they guard rather than fight against the nations they disapproved of. That's another story for another time.

I won't get into the politics and logistics of my thought process at that time because regardless of my experience, I still respect the warrior spirit carried by those who choose to fight in any environment for the greater good.

It happens to be the archetype I was gifted with, only now I choose my battles more wisely because it needed to evolve in my personal case.

Thankfully, I didn't see actual combat during my term. I was still able to fight for others instead of against them, in the sense of providing humanitarian efforts and disaster relief with my assigned unit. With that said, the one thing I'll credit the orchestrated chaos of military life with is the fact I learned more about myself than I ever could have in any classroom setting and did so very quickly.

It allowed me to sharpen my instincts by seeing what men and women were capable of when faced with the idea of survival and potentially having to trade bullets with an enemy they'll never meet face to face.

I learned to develop all of my senses and at the same time recognize the magnitude of my physical and mental capabilities. During this chapter of my journey, I became acquainted for the first time with my inner shadow. It was interesting that despite being exposed to the violence, injustice and other horrors of the outside world, none of them matched the greatest enemy of them all: myself.

My shadow presented itself under the guise of substance abuse; primarily alcohol.

What started as a fun weekend activity with friends and fellow warriors quickly turned into a downward spiral of lonesome, daily consumption to cope with unresolved stress and depression. Liquor bottles and beer cans lined the floors of just about every place I dared to call a proper home. It nearly obliterated my relationships with my family and friends time after time again.

Funny and kind of sad to say that even the old flings I had back then, which meant nothing to me to begin with, riddled me with feelings of guilt and shame for bringing them harm in the process of my poisoning.

My family and friends were always there for me when I needed them. What's ironic here is that while I had the courage to fight anything that was thrown at me by things outside of my control, I didn't have the courage to ask for help.

And that's because fighting was all I knew how to do. I never learned the art of retreat. After dealing with the consequences of my actions for long enough, I decided to finally accept defeat and surrender to the fact I may never win against this particular demon. Once I accepted this, I began my long recovery.

This strategy would test my patience like no other.

For every step forward, I took three steps back.
Old demons would resurface to taunt me and entice me to escape to the bottom of the bottle every time. "One last time" became more expensive each day and not just because I spent money that I couldn't afford to waste on a habit that's not even worth a cent. It became expensive in the sense that I was paying for this with the two things that no worldly currency could ever afford to repay me with: time and health.

I've spoken with many other people who experienced this type of battle and similar ones over the course of my recovery. It was through sharing our personal experiences that we were able to help each other out more than trying to battle this alone.

I found it interesting that most of them described their experience as train-wrecks, car crashes, and other sudden events that all led to a point of self-destruction. My perspective was a bit different than getting caught in fiery blazes and mangled steel. For me, it was more like being on a ship which was slowly sinking in the middle of an ocean infested with creatures of the deep; waiting for their food to fall in.

It was a slow surrender.

Jumping overboard would save me from a long and drawn-out death awaiting me by allowing the beasts beneath me to consume me much quicker and end my self-inflicted suffering.

Alternatively, I could've remained onboard, yet the end would've been the same nonetheless. At first glance, there was simply no escape.

I knew very well how this story would end if I didn't participate in my own rescue. Action was needed from my part, and it was action that would take immense amounts of courage from me at that time.

So I searched for answers every waking moment as my metaphorical ship slowly sank. I wanted this battle to be over as quickly as possible. Therefore, I read books on the subject to help myself, asked for the right guidance from friends, family, I even went to church seeking help, watched hundreds of videos, I spoke to counselors, doctors, tried to quit cold turkey, etc.

You name it and I probably gave it a semi-decent try.

I tried practically everything except checking myself into a long-term rehabilitation facility because I didn't really see the purpose of it. Not to mention, given that I was in crippling debt due to my poor spending habits at the time, I also couldn't afford to see any more professionals. I lacked the patience I needed to dig deeper in my search for answers. I was underestimating the enemy and not appreciating my allies.

The worst of all, I was acting like a coward thinking that this monster would consume me.

After continuously trying to drink my problems away and ending up in the ER more times than I care to admit, I eventually hit the absolute lowest point of my life.

I had fallen face-first into the mouth of madness. The previous vision of the sinking ship became a burning castle...

Sound familiar?

It was at this point when I thought that I had lost it all. I thought I lost every opportunity to have a healthy relationship with my family and friends.

I thought I would lose all of my material belongings and my job. Even my will to live seemed to be completely lost; I grew tired of fighting and making enemies where friends should be. Whatever force I was fighting against had won and I admitted true defeat. I thought I'd never recover again.

I'll spare you the grim details, but there was a particular point along this inferno when I found myself hallucinating while blacking in and out of consciousness in an empty room. No light, no sounds, only the shadows in the corners creeping up to take me away. I thought this would be the end of the road for me, and they probably would take me away for good.

It was at that split-second moment when I recognized that the hell I found myself was inescapable and it was the consequence of my own actions. By accepting this outcome and not running from it anymore, it was right then how I took back the power that was stolen from me. Courage began to take shape.

I recognized that by making this far, after so many years of struggling, I knew that night wasn't my time to go and I could go further.

Although my survival would be of the utmost importance, I knew it would be just as difficult as the battle itself; meaning I would fall again sooner or later.

However, I also knew that after each failure there would be a greater victory ahead of me.

This is how I learned to no longer fight against the current; I fought alongside it. The flame ignited by my passion to live, to love and to share stories with the world became so immense, that I knew that sooner or later I would defeat this and I would do the impossible by breaking down the gates of this burning castle.

The periods of recovery were often sporadic but I was grateful for them and their increased frequency regardless.

Whenever I would slip and indulge my demons, I did so knowing the potential outcome of my actions.
Going through with these strange wagers with the devil meant that some of the time I would lose, but most of the time I would win.

"Who wins against the devil", you ask? After all, the devil is a clever one. So who better to outwit the devil than the devil himself? This is how I came to understand that becoming a monster in order to tame the other is critical. That is because the sense of direction and the meaning behind each of our battles is very different. My downfalls would become my strength and used for the greater good.

My fighting chance exposed itself by the fact I spent enough time in that hell to know every crevice, every trap and every painful obstacle that would set me back. There was nothing left to surprise me, only strengthen me.
The moment closest to my demise was the moment I was able to see the true extent of my bravery.

I weighed all the risks against the benefits each time. I came to understand that I wouldn't win this fight if it was for just myself. I had to use my passion to live for the other people who loved me. I used my understanding of the consequences of my actions to prepare myself for the greater victory that followed each tumble along the path.

Ultimately, when I used courage to retreat, I was able to reach a vantage point where I owned my demons and the damage they were causing me and others around me. By accepting responsibility for my actions, I had finally rooted my tree in the hell I was in; knowing it would one day branch out and grow towards heaven.

This was one of the most powerful lessons in courage I learned and one I've been waiting to share with the world hoping to inspire someone who is also struggling with their own personal demons, no matter what they may be.

Personally, it took courage to surrender to the fact that I wasn't in a position to win. To recognize that I was outnumbered, outsmarted, and outmaneuvered each time I tried to plot my escape. Courage in my case wasn't about overcoming the challenge from one day to the next, it was about enduring it.

I came to the realization that I'll never encounter challenges that I couldn't one day overcome or learn something from. I had to be comfortable with looking in the mirror and thank the worst version of myself for allowing me to see what I'm capable of doing.

As well as granting me a glimpse of what other people are capable of doing when they're in the clutches of their own shadows.

In short, by seeing the worst of me I was able to let the best of me shine through and break free from the flames that almost consumed me. Now that I consider them a part of me, I use them to light the way for myself and others to unleash our best selves.

Centering back in on the topic of courage, by no means should you go out and purposely find the thing that hurts you or others and exploit it to its extremes. Believe me when I say that in many cases, it'll find you first. If you're currently living in a time of inner peace, consider yourself fortunate; even blessed.

Just be mindful that sooner or later, something will come along to challenge you. Thus, you should patiently prepare the best you can for when it comes and be grateful for where you currently find yourself and whom you find yourself with in these calm times.

There's no point in rushing out to seek danger. Your only task is to be ready in the areas you can control for when it eventually shows up. That is your body, your mind and your spirit.

It should go without say that causing yourself or others more harm than is needed for the sake of enduring a fight is also not always the best solution. I was fortunate in my case, but your battle is going to be unique to your environment, your age, your mindset, and many other factors. Therefore, your strategy and the answer to your victory won't be the same as mine.

If you have the resources, use them. If the help is available, take it when you can. The ego must go. While it has its uses, more often than not, the ego is only able to carry you so far in dangerous situations like the one I described.

Like the war generals of olden times, knowing when to tactically retreat is just as important as the fight itself. The purpose of it being: to survive complete annihilation and be able to fight one more day.

Lastly, when you eventually land in the deepest and darkest corners of your inner shadow, it's important that you see it for what it is and not give it more power than it deserves by hiding from it. Whether that's issues with communication, gambling, punctuality, a bad temper, your spending habits or anything that's interfering with your current quality of life.

The more you try to repress it, the more it'll continue to try to break free and end up destroying you.

What you resist will persist. If you run, it'll chase. You must stand your ground, accept it for what it is and be brave when facing it.

When these challenges present themselves, you must take back control. Like gratification, it doesn't have to happen immediately. It's possible to get caught with your guard down sometimes and you may find yourself falling. As long as you keep your eyes on the target and have the willingness to continue, you can turn all weaknesses into strengths and use them in your favor.

Through courage, you'll see each personal challenge or conflict you cross in life as a means to develop how you control yourself and how you can regain control of the situation that's trying to harm you.

Taking the necessary meaningful action and understanding the consequences of all that you do in the face of chaos is exactly how you can get a better grasp of your inner shadows. When you channel your inner shadow to aid you in life as opposed to letting it destroy you, that doesn't mean it'll disappear forever. It'll always be a part of you.

All it means is that it's no longer the thing in complete charge of your actions or in control of your outcomes.

Finally, if your demons can handled with ease, handle them. Don't wait until they get worse. If they're already consuming you, recognize their power and stand down. I don't mean stand down as "giving up" completely. Giving up is not an option.

What I mean is that surrendering through acceptance to gain a different perspective and create a new path to ultimate victory can be as beautiful as the thrill of the fight itself.

Always be brave in your approach and always choose your battles wisely. If they happen to choose you, well, now you have an idea of what it takes to come out victorious.

Courage Takeaways

◆ **Adversity is the easiest way to breed courage.** Adversity requires both offensive and defensive tactics. Expose yourself to the challenges that life offers you so that you may be ready for the greatest test of your character and bravery when the time comes.

◆ **Courage doesn't always have to be loud and proud.** The wars you'll fight are sometimes silent in reference to your victories and losses. This doesn't make them any less worthy of taking on or sharing with others in a modest way. You give power to the fight you're in.

◆ **Everyone is fighting a hard battle but it matters how you express yourself.** Speak your truth with honesty and kindness. You must use the lessons that courage teaches to benefit you and your community. If you're in a place of strength, remember to help the weak. If you're in a place of weakness, you can still inspire those weaker than you to trudge forward.

◆ **Courage isn't always born from chaos.** It can show up in the form of giving and receiving love, sharing a deep secret or being graceful when it isn't called for. Acts of kindness in a cruel world are as courageous as engaging in any kind of combat; whether internal or external.

◆ **Courage doesn't mean you're fearless.** Acknowledging your fears is the first step in breeding courage. Seeing your fears for what they are and not aggrandizing them, you'll realize how brightly your passion burns and how rewarding the consequences can be.

◆ **Courage is taking decisive action.** Take meaningful action in a direction that's best suited for you and those around you. Even in times when tough choices must be made, staying true to what fuels your fire is far better than acting blindly or fearfully. Fear is a great warning system, but that's about where the benefits end. Courage is limitless.

Completing The Circle

The universe is constantly changing and people will adapt.

With the amount of information you have available to you, it makes it too easy to educate yourself on the various things that life has to offer. Unless you're reading this book in some dystopian future years after its creation, then things might not be so easy.

All joking aside, this method can work for you regardless of your environment. You only need yourself and the willingness to be the best version of yourself.

Let's not forget that the amount of information out there can ensnare you in an endless loop of thought. It makes it easy to be fooled and overwhelmed by the amount of things you think you have to keep up with.

You may be asking how patience, gratitude and courage apply to other virtues and characteristics. The reality is that these three values are ones that you can use as foundations rather than end goals. They are paths you can follow to lead you to a particular finish line in life, big or small.

In other words, each one of these values acts as its own large tree with hundreds of thousands of its own branches. Each one yielding its own type of leaves, fruits and things of that nature.

This means that regardless of the mountains you hope to one day conquer in your life, if your eyes are stuck on the summit you won't know if the path you walk along is right for you. Thus, these three foundations will help you stay aligned, prevent you from getting lost and can always act as a retreat should everything else fail at some point or another.

To put it simply, patience, gratitude and courage are indispensable steps in all aspects of your life. I believe you'll benefit greatly from basing every choice you make on these three faculties.

Knowing where you'd like to be is easy. There are many people out there who are more than willing to help you reach those goals and will always point you in that direction. They may even walk alongside you. The difficult part is knowing where to start.

For instance, after this you may realize you want to become more productive during your daily life. You may want to become the kind of lover or spouse that you think your partner deserves. Perhaps your goa is a bit simpler than that, maybe all you want to do is decide what you'd like to eat for dinner.

No matter what your goals for the day or your goals for your lifetime, always remember that any journey to the top of any mountain should begin with patience, gratitude and courage.

You must also understand that there's no specific arrangement or sequence for the integration of these values.

You'll run into situations that simply won't allow you to be as patient, such as you or someone else being in immediate danger. There will be days when you feel there's simply nothing to be thankful for. There will be situations that will frighten or confuse you, therefore courage won't be instantly available, causing you to freeze or react impulsively, which may cause more harm than good.

As much as some people might argue against this, there's simply no schedule for life and you are, after all, only human. Virtually anything can happen to you at any given moment, even after this paragraph is done registering in your mind.

Life by its very nature is untimely and this is exactly why it's so strangely appealing. In spite of the many pitfalls we find along the way, subconsciously we're attracted to the unpredictable. The fact that every rising sun and waning moon might just surprise you for better or worse and nothing will change that is as thrilling as it is dangerous.

Sure, you may be at the mercy of time and gravity. But if there's one thing that is just as true as that, is the fact you have more power than you think.

You're far more capable to help yourself and others and it doesn't have to be as complicated as others make it out to be.

Just because the complexity of people is its own type of undisputed beast doesn't mean you have to carry that weight on your shoulders or even mimic it. Hence, your only concern is to focus on the three values, should you choose to do so.

I say choose because, of course, this isn't a bulletproof method.

You might be wanting to discard everything I've shared with you and be on your own merry way as you've always have before. Life will carry on, you'll experience the same joys, the same chaos and the same little nothings of every day life. If you're content with that, then wonderful.

I'll remind you that the purpose of patience, gratitude and courage isn't for you to discard every thing you already know or not know. As I mentioned in the beginning, this can either be the introduction to a perspective you may not have considered before or a reinforcement to what you're already living day to day. It's meant to show you where your personal characteristics should be rooted. To be a better version of yourself, this is how you can begin and everything else that is meant to follow along will come along.

If it's meant for you, the river will bring it.

There are several other great traits you'll want to master and the information is out there for you to find.

I'll say, you won't be too surprised to learn that you must include patience, gratitude and courage in all things. Such as demonstrating respect, having good manners, becoming a better lover, a better friend, a more diligent worker, showing integrity and hundreds more.

If life has become far too chaotic for you and it's simplicity you seek along your path, you can always return to these three values to think and act again in accordance with your destiny.

So even though you're only human and this isn't a bulletproof method, humans are also capable of doing incredible things. Being "only human" isn't a free pass to do what you want without taking others and the consequences of your actions, or lack thereof, into consideration.

This isn't to say the goal of this method is for you to never make mistakes or you needing to be perfect. All you need is a simpler foundation.

A foundation that anyone who's willing is able to adopt, nurture and master. This is to prevent getting lost in the noise of misdirection.

In the worst cases, perhaps you may be skeptical of the method or just don't care to be a better person. That's perfectly fine. Understand that the universe is perfectly balanced, so what you give is what you get.
If you choose to mirror others in their moments of weakness, it's precisely that which you wi l receive.

If you choose to be hateful, then hate will find you. If you won't forgive, then you won't be forgiven. If you latch on to detrimental emotions such as fear, jea ousy or greed, that's exactly what will become your own burning castle.

Thankfully, this flows both ways. If you give love, then love you shall receive. If you are wi ling to help others, then others will eventually help you. Kindness, compassion, respect, selflessness and all other traits found in people will either be founded on patience, gratitude and courage - or their absence.

In closing and with absolute confidence, I can say that by understanding patience, you can see the world through a softer heart and a clearer mind. You'll find not only stillness, but be able to flow instead of moving in undesired directions impulsively.

When you understand gratitude, the changes that take place in your mind will allow you to mo d an otherwise inflexible world to serve you, not harm you.

It will allow you to express yourself beautifully in situations that others consider terrible. It'll lessen the weight you needlessly carry on your shoulders.

Finally, courage will let you overcome any and all adversity. You'll turn your shadows into allies, as well take subsequent action that's meaningful.

Best of all, you'll be the pillar when others need support, the tree when others seek shade, and the hero of your own journey despite being a villain somewhere else.

You'll unlock the infinite force that every human on this planet is meant to use for good. Perfectly imperfect, divinely balanced and at peace with the choices that will tell the tale of your own life for years to come.

Who I Am

Sword&Ink is the pen name. Luigino Taboada Queirolo is the true name.

For as long as I can remember, I've had a passion for words and often found myself searching for answers to the mysteries of life. Unfortunately, I looked in all the wrong places along my own path and it brought me a great deal of challenges. I wrote this to help people understand that things don't have to be as complicated as they make them out to be. Because of the choices I've made in times of blind rage, weakness, confusion and more, I'm very well versed in the language of chaos. Therefore, I took it upon myself to learn why people do the things they do, why things happened the way that they did and developed this philosophy of my own.

It has helped me out tremendously across all categories of my life and I hope that it can help you all the same. Even if it doesn't, I wish it unlocks any deeply rooted thoughts you may have had about the multiple challenges you currently face or are getting ready to face.

I encourage you to apply this whenever you can, but also remember that it's not meant to be perfect. It's not the only solution out there. Use this in contrast or in conjunction with anything else of value you may have learned.

Most important of all, I hope you enjoyed reading this as much as I enjoyed writing it. Thank you once more and I wish you great success along your path.

Godspeed and God bless.